A+
books

WORLD OF COLORS

India in Colors

by Nathan Olson

Consultant: Rachel M. Heilman, member
The Association for Asian Studies

Capstone press

Mankato, Minnesota

Black and *orange* Bengal tigers roam the forests of India. They are protected in national parks and reserves. Bengal tigers hunt at night. Dark stripes help them hide in the shadows.

Colorful shades of **brown** and **red** spices tempt shoppers at markets in India. Spices like cinnamon, ginger, and garlic are used in many Indian dishes. India is a world leader in producing spices.

Green rice fields cover large areas of land in India. Rice is India's most important crop. It is often picked by hand. Many families depend on rice farming for their incomes. Only China grows more rice than India.

Hindus light **golden** lamps during Diwali. Diwali is the Hindu festival of lights. Hindus celebrate Diwali in October or November. They decorate their homes and temples with lamps. Families also gather together to exchange gifts and watch fireworks.

India is famous for fine silk fabrics in **red** and other bright colors. Weavers also make colorful cloth from cotton and wool. India's fabrics are sold to countries around the world.

These Indian women wear **red**, **yellow**, and **blue** saris. A sari is a long piece of cloth. Women wrap the cloth around their bodies to make dresses. The loose-fitting cloth helps them stay cool in hot weather.

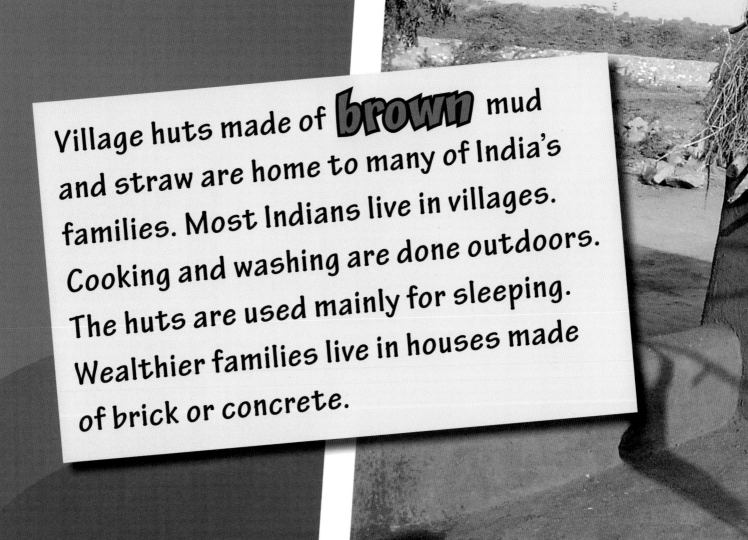

Village huts made of **brown** mud and straw are home to many of India's families. Most Indians live in villages. Cooking and washing are done outdoors. The huts are used mainly for sleeping. Wealthier families live in houses made of brick or concrete.

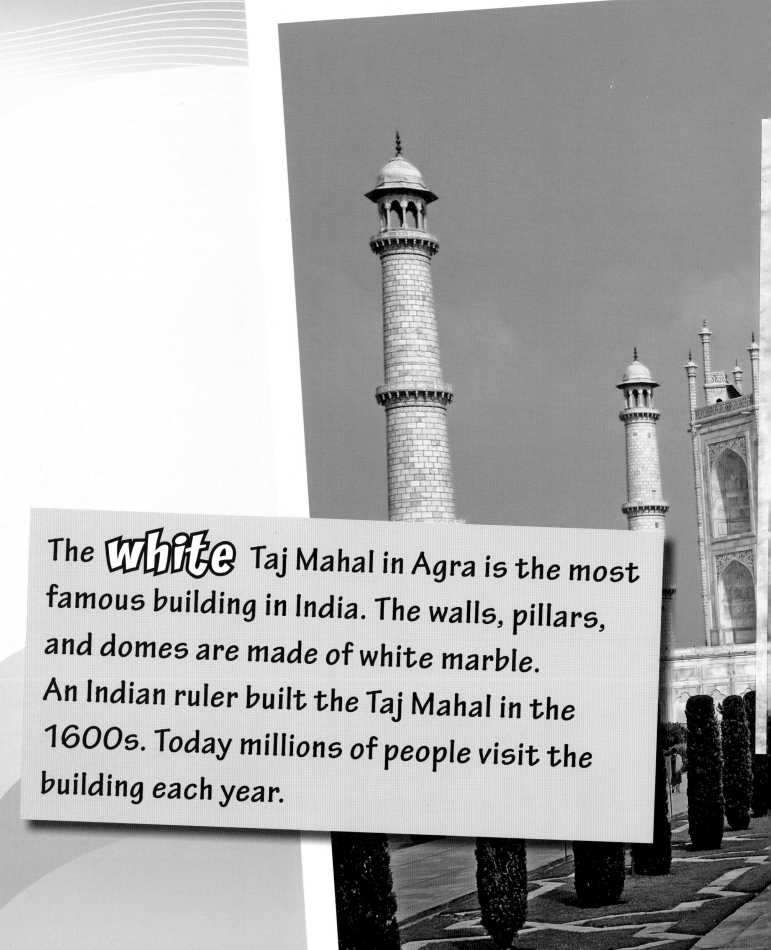

The **white** Taj Mahal in Agra is the most famous building in India. The walls, pillars, and domes are made of white marble. An Indian ruler built the Taj Mahal in the 1600s. Today millions of people visit the building each year.

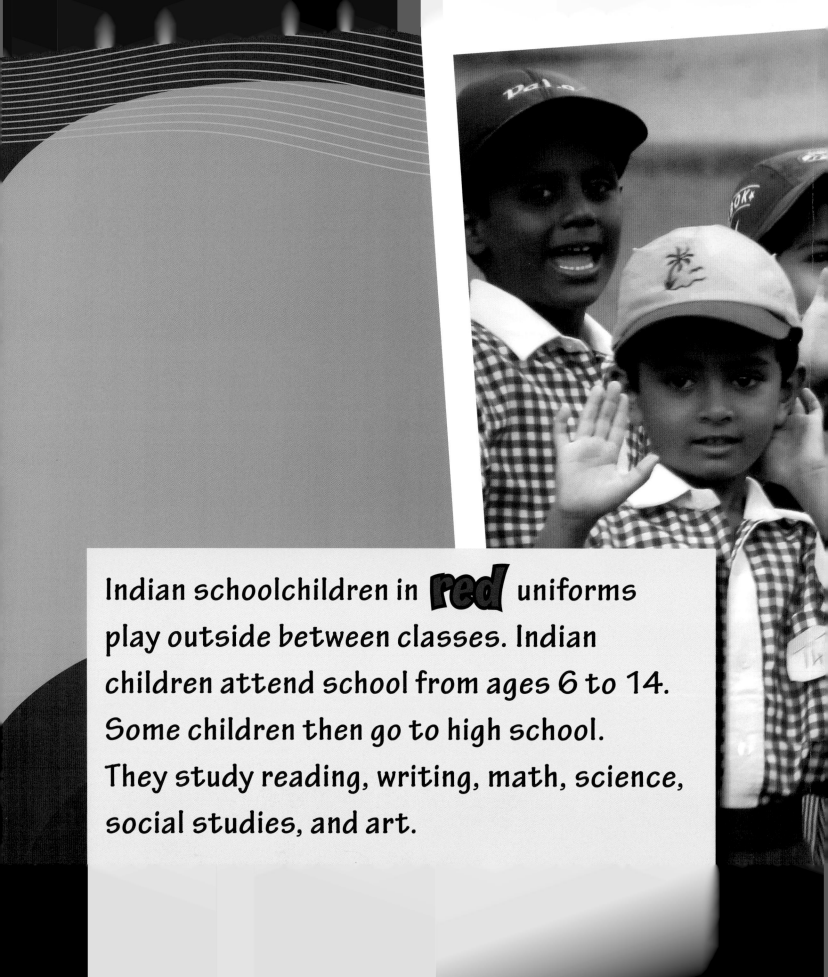

Indian schoolchildren in **red** uniforms play outside between classes. Indian children attend school from ages 6 to 14. Some children then go to high school. They study reading, writing, math, science, social studies, and art.

The **blue** water of the Arabian Sea borders the city of Mumbai. Mumbai is the biggest city in India. About 12 million people live there. Mumbai is also India's most important port.

An Indian man dressed in **purple** practices *gatka*. He spins a shield called a *chakkar*. Gatka is a type of martial art. Gatka demonstrations are popular at festivals and celebrations.

Pink and **orange** light brightens the Ganges River in northeastern India. The Ganges is the most important river in India. It makes nearby land rich for growing rice and other crops.

India's most famous leader stands as a shimmering **golden** statue. Mohandas Gandhi helped India become an independent country. He was a gentle man who practiced peace and patience.

FACTS about India

Capital City: New Delhi

Population: 1,147,995,904

Official Language: Hindi

Common Phrases

English	Hindi	Pronunciation
hello and good-bye	namaste	(nah-mah-STAY)
yes	haan	(HAH)
no	nahin	(nah-HEE)
thank you	dhanyavad	(done-yah-VAHD)

Map

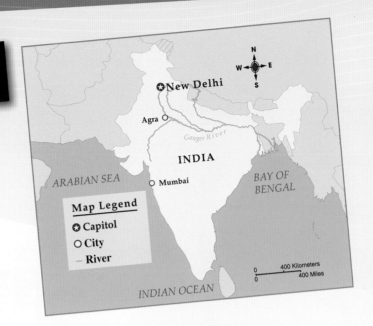

Flag

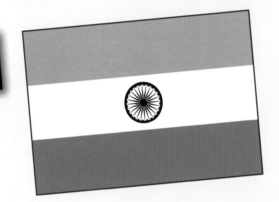

Money

Indian money is called the Indian rupee. One rupee equals 100 paise.

Glossary

Diwali (dee-VAH-lee) — the Hindu festival of lights

dome (DOHM) — a round roof

fabric (FAB-rik) — cloth or a soft material

gatka (GAHT-kuh) — a martial art using a sword and shield

Hindu (HIN-doo) — a person who practices the religion of Hinduism; Hindus believe that they must live in harmony with universal laws.

marble (MAR-buhl) — hard stone with colored patterns; people use marble for making buildings and statues.

port (PORT) — a harbor where ships dock safely

reserve (ree-ZURV) — a place set aside for animals to live

sari (SAH-ree) — a long piece of cloth that is wrapped around a woman's body

spice (SPISSE) — something used to flavor foods

temple (TEM-puhl) — a building used for worship

Read More

Aboff, Marcie. *India ABCs: A Book about the People and Places of India.* Country ABCs. Minneapolis: Picture Window Books, 2006.

Hardyman, Robyn. *Celebrate India.* Celebrate. New York: Chelsea Clubhouse, 2009.

Parker, Victoria. *We're from India.* We're From. Chicago: Heinemann, 2005.

Internet Sites

FactHound offers a safe, fun way to find educator-approved Internet sites related to this book.

Here's what you do:

1. Visit www.facthound.com

2. Choose your grade level.

3. Begin your search.

This book's ID number is 9781429622233.

FactHound will fetch the best sites for you!

Index

A+ Books are published by Capstone Press,
151 Good Counsel Drive, P.O. Box 669, Mankato, Minnesota 56002.
www.capstonepress.com

1 2 3 4 5 6 14 13 12 11 10 09

Library of Congress Cataloging-in-Publication Data
Olson, Nathan.
 India in colors / by Nathan Olson.
 p. cm. — (A+ books. World of colors)
 Includes bibliographical references and index.
 Summary: "Simple text and striking photographs present India, its culture,
and its geography" — Provided by publisher.
 ISBN-13: 978-1-4296-2223-3 (hardcover)
 ISBN-10: 1-4296-2223-7 (hardcover)
 1. India — Juvenile literature. 2. India — Pictorial works — Juvenile literature. I. Title.
II. Series.
DS407.O4724 2009   2008034129
954 — dc22

Credits

Megan Peterson, editor; Veronica Bianchini, set designer; Kyle Grenz, book designer;
    Wanda Winch, photo researcher

Photo Credits

Alamy/Imagebroker/Urs Schweitzer, 22–23; Alamy/James Cheadle, 27; Art Life
Images/Icarus/IML/Meazza, cover; DigitalVision, 2–3; Doranne Jacobson, 6–7, 10,
13, 19, 24–25; Newscom/PPI Photo/Imran Ali, 8; Peter Arnold/sinopictures, 20–21;
Shutterstock/Andrew Chin, 29 (flag); Shutterstock/Jeremy Richards, 4–5; Shutterstock/
Sid B. Viswakumar, 29 (money); Shutterstock/Taolmor, 1, 16–17; Shutterstock/Vishal
Shah, 14–15

Note to Parents, Teachers, and Librarians
This World of Colors book uses full-color photographs and a nonfiction format
to introduce children to basic topics in the study of countries. *India in Colors* is
designed to be read aloud to a pre-reader or to be read independently by an
early reader. Photographs help listeners and early readers understand the text
and concepts discussed. The book encourages further learning by including the
following sections: Facts about India, Glossary, Read More, Internet Sites, and
Index. Early readers may need assistance using these features.